故園畫憶

庚寅中秋

韩启德题

故园画忆系列

Memory of the Old Home in Sketches

葫芦岛印迹

Traces of Huludao City

范贻光等　绘画
侯　铁　王云刚　撰文

Sketches by Fan Yiguang and others
Notes by Hou Tie, Wang Yungang

學苑出版社
Academy Press

图书在版编目（CIP）数据

葫芦岛印迹 / 范贻光等绘；侯铁，王云刚撰．—北京：学苑出版社，2011.12

（故园画忆系列）

ISBN 978-7-5077-3917-6

Ⅰ．①葫…　Ⅱ．①范…　②侯…　③王…　Ⅲ．①葫芦岛市－概况－图集

Ⅳ．①K923.13-64

中国版本图书馆CIP数据核字(2011)第258974号

绘　画：范贻光　于名川　李承毅

　　　　张廷禄　赵文涛

撰　文：侯　铁　王云刚

出 版 人：孟　白

出版发行：学苑出版社

社　　址：北京市丰台区南方庄2号院1号楼

邮政编码：100079

网　　址：www.book001.com

电子信箱：xueyuan@public.bta.net.cn

销售电话：010-67675512、67678944、67601101（邮购）

印 刷 厂：高碑店市鑫宏源印刷有限责任公司

开本尺寸：889×1194　1/24

印　　张：5

字　　数：80千字

图　　幅：82幅

版　　次：2011年12月第1版

印　　次：2011年12月第1次印刷

定　　价：28.00元

走廊四百里　文化六千年

一位年近古稀的老人，十几次奔波在人迹罕至的崇山峻岭，去探究辽宁境内明代长城的历史文化渊源；本该颐养天年，却不停地东奔西走，四处寻访，查阅资料，只求弄明白安特生如何发现了六千年前葫芦岛市南票区沙锅屯的红山文化遗址。这位执著的文化学者、画家，就是原《中华文化画报》的主编范贻光先生。我们这部书三分之二的作品，出自于范先生之手，余下之作，是应范先生之邀来葫芦岛创作的国内著名画家（几位画家均为范先生五十多年前中央美院附中的同窗学友）所绘。

作为身居北京的艺术家，对葫芦岛历史文化的热衷，几乎到了痴迷的程度，令我感动和敬佩。从某种意义上讲，范先生已经把葫芦岛视为第二故乡了。大半生从事历史文化研究的范先生，对全国很多地方的文化遗产如数家珍。退休之后，各地争相聘请他为该地编辑文化专辑，而范先生却对葫芦岛情有独钟，时常徜徉于葫芦岛的历史长河中而不能自拔，并最终与学苑出版社共同促成了这部作品的问世，成为承载中华民族传统文化的《故园画忆》系列图书之一。

据我所知，像范先生这样的一批学者与艺术家们，之所以对葫芦岛流连忘返，是因为其独特而险要的地理位置，多民族的交融与变迁，记载着太多的历代王朝的兴与衰，留下了太多的民族心灵的伤与痛。

葫芦岛六个县（市）区，大部分位于“扼山海之要冲，为京师之屏障”的辽西走廊，地处山海关至锦州的狭长沿海平原地带。这里背山面海，是沟通东三省与关内的咽喉，历来为兵家必争之地。四百里的走廊就是一部浩繁的史卷，承载着中华民族沉重的历史。从沙锅屯原始人类的刀耕火种，到春秋战国时期遍布的墓葬遗迹；从秦始皇东巡碣石宫虔诚地求仙，到曹操北征乌桓留下的“东临碣石，以观沧海”；从辽金元跌宕起伏的民族纷争，到明亡清兴六十年的风雨变幻；从民国初年的两次直奉大战，到塔山阻击战为新中国奠定基业……葫芦岛的每一块土地，都留下了难以磨灭的文化印痕。

本书从明代古城、绥中长城、历史脉络、名胜探幽四部分入手，以古城、长城为点，以葫芦岛的历史沿革和名胜古迹的分布为线，两点两线地架构起本书的主框架。书中融入了画家们独特的审美与发现，形象细致地绘制了葫芦岛的历史文化风貌，给世间留下了一笔丰厚的精神财富。在此，我谨代表葫芦岛市人民，向各位画家、作者，向学苑出版社致以诚挚的谢意。

翻过厚重的历史，如今的葫芦岛如同一颗渤海明珠，镶嵌在蓝色的绕海玉带上。四百里的长廊，国道102线、京沈高速公路、京哈铁路、秦沈高速铁路，与沿海开放的滨海大道，构成了一道多彩的五线谱，等待着您拨出动听的音符。

东北的大门向您敞开，关外第一市葫芦岛，随时准备拥抱您。

孙兆林（葫芦岛市市委书记）

2011年11月

Four Hundred *Li* Corridor Six Thousand Years of Culture

Mr. Fan Yiguang, former Chief Editor of *Chinese Culture Magazine,* visited the isolated mountainous area in Liaoning Province more than ten times to explore the history and cultural origin of the Ming Great Wall. In his late sixties, an age when most people expect to have a relaxed lifestyle, he traveled to many places and carried out numerous interviews in his endless research. He was on a quest to reveal the story of how Anderson discovered the site of Hongshan Culture in the vicinity of Shaguotun near the city of Huludao.

Two thirds of the art in this book is the work of Mr. Fan, with the remainder being works of famous artists who had been classmates of Fan 50 years ago at the High School Attached to Central Academy of Fine Arts and who had been invited by him to work in Huludao.

I much admire Mr. Fan's passion for the history and culture of Huludao. Although he lives in Beijing, he looks upon Huludao as his second home town. It is not surprising that Mr. Fan has a comprehensive knowledge of Chinese heritage for he has devoted most of his life to historical research and study. After retirement, he was invited by many regional organizations across the country to compile articles about their local culture. However, he cannot help indulging his fascination for the rich history of Huludao. The fruit of his passion is this book which is included in the book series *Memory of the Old Home in Sketches,* published by Academy Press.

With its distinguished geographical features and historically crucial location, Huludao has witnessed many changes and the intermingling of multiple ethnic groups and their cultures. Over thousands of years the people of this part of China have witnessed the rise and fall, the glory and decline of many dynasties, often resulting in tears and wounded hearts. This is probably the very reason that Huludao attracts Mr. Fan and other scholars and artists.

Most of Huludao City's six districts are located along the Western Liaoning Corridor where the meeting of the mountains and the sea serves as a natural barrier for protecting the capital. Huludao is located on a flat strip of land between the sea front and the mountains. A corridor of land between Shanhaiguan City and Jinzhou City is the throat for entering into Shanhaiguan pass from the Northeast. Historically, this has made it a place of strategic importance and many battles have been fought in this area.

The 400 *li* Western Liaoning Corridor is like a great book of the long history of Chinese people. From the prehistoric human activities of Shaguotun to the tombs of the Spring and Autumn Period (722 B.C.-481 B.C.); from Qin Shihuang's visit to the Jieshi Palace to worship the Gods, to Cao Cao's famous poem written on his north-bound journey when he led a force match deep into Wuhuan territory; from ethnic strife in period of the Liao, Jin and Yuan dynasties, to the 60 years period of war that ended with the Qing Dynasty (1616-1911) replacing the Ming Dynasty (1368-1644); from the two Zhili-Fengtian Wars in the early republican period, to the Tashan Battle during the War of Liberation, which helped lay the foundations for the New China, all left indelible marks in this corridor.

This book has four sections: *Historic Towns of the Ming Dynasty, The Suizhong Great Wall, Veins of History,* and *Exploration of Historic Sites*. The framework of the book woven with two veins being the history of Huludao and the distribution of historic sites, while the historic towns and The Great Wall are incorporated like two knots to strengthen it. The artists' works reveal their personal aesthetic discovery of the area and portray the history and culture of Huludao, and will surely be a source of spiritual wealth for generations to come. I'd like to thank the artists, the writers and Academy Press on behalf of the Huludao people.

Having turned the heavy page of history, Huludao today is like a sparkling pearl on the blue ribbon of Bohai Bay. The 400 *li* Corridor, National Road No.102, Beijing-Shenyang Expressway, Beijing-Harbin Railway, Qinhuangdao-Shenyang High Speed Railway and the road along the Sea Front, are as blank music sheets awaiting your composition.

Known as the first city outside Shanhaiguan Pass, Huludao is an open doorway to the Northeast, with arms ready to give you a welcoming embrace.

Sun Zhaolin

(Secretary of the CPC Huludao Municipal Committee)

Nov. 2011

目　录

明代古城 1
兴城古城平面图 2
兴城古城城墙 3
兴城春和门 4
兴城延辉门 5
俯视小月城 6
兴城古城马道 7
兴城古城魁星楼 8
兴城古城钟鼓楼 9
文庙圆洞门上的砖雕图案 10
从棂星门旁的门洞望第二进院 11
兴城文庙棂星门 12
文庙第二进院的状元桥 13
文庙的古松 14
卧桐成林 15
大成殿 16
祖大乐的石牌坊（从北望去） 17
祖大寿的石牌坊（从南望去） 18
祖大乐石牌坊下的石狮子 19
前所古城 20
前所古城西门瓮城 21
觉华岛囤粮城遗址 22

绥中长城 23
绥中长城各段落名称示意图 24
九门口长城（一） 25
九门口长城（二） 26
九门口闸门 27
庙山口长城 28
夕阳口长城 29
夕阳口长城残破的敌台 30
黄土岭长城 31
甘城子长城 32
吾名口关关门 33
蓟镇长城南线 34
锥子山以南蓟镇长城 35
金匣沟长城 36
敌楼 37
小河口长城第2段砖墙 38
小河口长城第6段砖石结构的墙体 39
西沟长城 40
西沟长城敌楼 41
大毛山长城 42
大毛山长城残破的敌台 43
锥子山长城（一） 44

锥子山长城（二） 45
椴木冲长城 46
蔓枝草长城 47
金牛洞长城 48
锥子山长城东段 49
三台子烽火台 50
夕阳口长城1号烽火台 51
敌台的墙体 52
小河口长城4号敌台 53
墙体（一） 54
墙体（二） 55
锥子山长城的山险及石墙 56
小河口一段山险 57
鼓山长城山险墙 58

历史脉络 **59**

沙锅屯洞穴遗址 60
绥中碣石宫（秦汉）遗址 61
寻觅碣石宫 62
前卫斜塔 63
沙锅屯石塔 64
兴城白塔峪塔 65
妙峰寺双塔 66
水下考古发现的元代瓷器 67
朱梅墓园 68
文化的交融 69
葫芦岛大遣返 70
塔山阻击战 71
葫芦岛和平宣言 72

名胜探幽 **73**

觉华岛俯瞰 74
觉华岛的海岸 75
觉华岛海边的渔船 76
大龙宫寺遗址 77
觉华岛的菩提树 78
唐王洞 79
遥望觉华岛唐王洞 80
莲花山圣水寺 81
圣水寺天元宫 82
圣水寺后山坡的一座院落 83
圣水寺碧云宫 84
灵山寺 85
天然寺 86

Contents

Historic Towns of the Ming Dynasty 1
Schematic Plan of Xingcheng Town 2
Walls of Xingcheng 3
The Chunhe Gate Tower of Xingcheng 4
The Yanhui Gate Tower of Xingcheng 5
A Bird's-eye View of the Xiaoyue Town 6
A Ramp of the City Wall in Xingcheng 7
The Kuixing Pavilion in Xingcheng 8
The Bell Tower in Xingcheng 9
Brick Carvings on the Arch of the Confucius Temple 10
View of the Second Courtyard from the Arch Beside the Lingxing Arch 11
The Lingxing Arch of the Confucius Temple in Xingcheng 12
The Zhuangyuan Bridge in the Second Courtyard of the Confucius Temple 13
Old Pine Tree in the Temple 14
A Forest from One Plane Tree 15
The Dacheng Hall 16
View of the Zu Dale Memorial Arch from the North 17
View of the Zu Dashou Memorial Arches from the South 18
Stone Lions under the Zu Dale Arch 19
The Historic Town of Qiansuo 20
Wengcheng (Barbican) of the West Gate of Qiangsuo 21
The Ruins of Army Supply Town on Juehua Island 22

The Suizhong Great Wall 23
The Plan of the Suizhong Great Wall 24
The Jiumenkou Great Wall (1) 25
The Jiumenkou Great Wall (2) 26
The Jiumenkou Lock Gate 27
The Miaoshankou Great Wall 28
The Xiyangkou Great Wall 29
Ruined Watchtower of the Xiyangkou Great Wall 30
The Huangtuling Great Wall 31
The Ganchengzi Great Wall 32
The Wumingkou Pass 33
South Stretch of the Jizhen Great Wall 34
The Jizhen Great Wall to the South of Zhuizi Mountain 35
The Jinxiagou Great Wall 36
A Watchtower of the Great Wall 37
The Second Segment of the Xiaohekou Great Wall 38
The Sixth Segment of the Xiaohekou Great Wall Features Brick and Stone Masonry Structure 39

The Xigou Great Wall 40
Watchtower at the Xigou Great Wall 41
The Damaoshan Great Wall 42
Ruined Watchtower at
the Damaoshan Great Wall 43
The Zhuizishan Great Wall (1) 44
The Zhuizishan Great Wall (2) 45
The Duanmuchong Great Wall 46
The Manzhicao Great Wall 47
The Jinniudong Great Wall 48
The East Section
of the Zhuizishan Great Wall 49
Santaizi Beacon Tower 50
No. 1 Beacon Tower of
the Xiyangkou Great Wall 51
The Walls of a Watchtower 52
No. 4 Watchtower of
the Xiaohekou Great Wall 53
The Wall (1) 54
The Wall (2) 55
The Stone Walls and the Natural Barrier of
Zhuizishan Great Wall 56
The "Mountain Wall" along
the Xiaohekou Great Wall 57
The "Mountain Wall" of Gushan 58

Veins of History 59
The Shaguotun Cave Site 60
The Suizhong Site of the Jieshi Palace
(Qin and Han Dynasty) 61
The Legend of Jieshi Palace 62
The Qianwei Leaning Pagoda 63
The Shaguotun Stone Pagoda 64
The Xingcheng Baitayu Pagoda 65
The Twin Pagodas in Miaofeng Mountain 66
Underwater Archeological Discovery:
Yuan Dynasty (1206-1368) Porcelain 67
Zhu Mei's Tomb 68
The Intermingling of Cultures 69
The Huludao Repatriation of the Japanese 70
The Tashan Battle 71
The Huludao Peace Declaration 72

Exploration of Historic Sites 73
Bird's-eye View of Juehua Islands 74
Coast of Juehua Island 75
Fishing Boats in the Sea Off Juehua Island 76
The Dalonggong Temple 77
The Bodhi Trees of Juehua Island 78
Tangwang Cave 79
View of Tangwang Cave, Juehua Island
from Afar 80
The Shengshui Temple on Lianhua Mountain 81
Tianyuan Hall of the Shengshui Temple 82
A Courtyard on the Hillside Behind
the Shengshui Temple 83
Biyun Hall of the Shengshui Temple 84
The Lingshan Temple 85
The Tianran Temple 86

明代古城

Historic Towns of the Ming Dynasty

葫芦岛市的明代古城包括兴城古城、绥中的前所古城和觉华岛的明代古城。

兴城古城是目前我国保存较完整的一座明代古城。创建于明宣德三年（1428 年），明代称宁远卫城，是当时的军事重镇。明清之战中的两次著名战役“宁远大捷”和“宁锦大捷”都发生在这里。

前所古城在绥中县前所镇。建于明宣德三年（1428 年），是辽东镇 127 座明代所城目前保存最好的一座，也是山海关外的第一座所城。

觉华岛明代古城，毁于清军多尔衮进岛屠城的行动中，现在只有古城的遗址。

Historic towns of the Ming Dynasty (1368-1644) in Huludao City include Xingcheng, Qiansuo of Suizhong , and the one of Juehua Island.

The historic town of Xingcheng is the best preserved. Founded in 1428, it was known as Ningyuan Weicheng and was of great military importance. “Ningyuan” and “Ningjin” are two well known battles that took place here during the Ming-Qing Wars.

Qiansuo, in Suizhong County, was founded in 1428, one of 127 historic towns built in the Ming Dynasty. It is the best preserved and also the first one outside the Shanhaiguan Pass.

The historical town of Juehua Island was destroyed by the Qing army in a slaughter and all that remains are the ruins.

兴城古城

兴城古城平面图

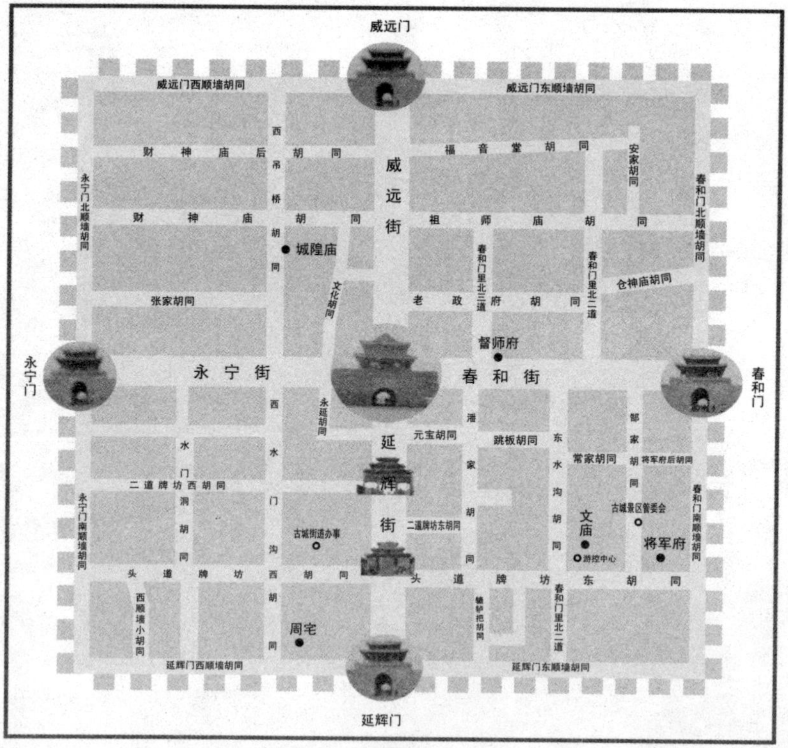

兴城古城，位于辽宁省兴城市，是我国目前保存最完整的四座明代古城之一，是唯一一座方形卫城。在42平方公里的区域内，集“城、泉、山、海、岛”五大景观于一体，珠联璧合，形成了北方沿海风景旅游区独特的风姿。

兴城古城背倚辽西丘陵，南临渤海，雄踞辽西走廊中部咽喉之地。是辽东地区通往中原的交通要道。辽圣宗统和八年（990年）始称兴城。明宣德三年（1428年），明政府在此设卫建城，赐名“宁远”。明代兴城古城称宁远卫城，清代称宁远州城，民国三年（1914年）重新启用兴城之名，延用至今。

城墙高10米，周长3274米，城墙外壁用大型灰青色长方砖砌筑，内壁用不规则块石垒砌，俗称“虎皮墙”。兴城古城为全国重点文物保护单位。城内正中有钟鼓楼一座，并有明代祖氏石坊和文庙等古迹。

明代，宁远古城为边防重地，明将袁崇焕驻兵于此，屡败清兵。天启六年（1626年）1月，清太祖努尔哈赤率兵13万围攻宁远城，身负重伤而败退。天启七年5月，清太祖统军再攻宁远城，再败于城下。

兴城古城以前分外城和内城，外城现已无存，内城经历代维修，基本保持原貌。城的四面正中皆有城门。城门外有半圆形瓮城。瓮城即城门外的小月城。

城墙设有东南西北四门：东曰春和；南曰延辉；西曰永宁；北曰威远。城门上各有两层楼阁、围廊式箭楼、坡形砌登道。城门外筑有半圆形瓮城，城墙四角筑有炮台，用来架设红夷大炮。城墙基砌青色条石，外砌大块青砖，内垒巨型块石，中间夹夯黄土。

Schematic Plan of Xingcheng Town

Located in Liaoning Province, the Historic Town of Xingcheng is one of four from the Ming Dynasty (1368-1644) and the only square-shaped town. Standing against the Liaoxi Mountains, with the Bohai Sea to the south, its vital location in the West-Liaoning Corridor makes it the gateway between East Liaoning and the Central Plains of China.

兴城古城城墙

Walls of Xingcheng

一段城墙就是一段战争史、一段发展史，像是壁立的长形丰碑，记录着朝代更叠的曲折与残酷，像是兵士的相拥队伍，上面排列着激烈战斗的血腥与惨烈——

兴城春和门

The Chunhe Gate Tower of Xingcheng

把历史画个圆，换个角度审视城垣。春和门饱经风霜的剥蚀、战火的洗礼——岿然如故。

兴城延辉门

The Yanhui Gate Tower of Xingcheng

城门，腥风血雨的见证者。目睹六百年的世事沧桑，目睹几个朝代的历史沿革，目睹数不清的悲欢离合。登斯楼，感慨万千。

俯视小月城

A Bird's-eye View of the Xiaoyue Town

瓮城是宁远古城的臂膀，也是护卫城池的一道防线。看到它，人们自然联想起“瓮中捉鳖”的故事。这里有过多少次厮杀没有人能计数；这里有过多少个可歌可泣的故事已不见史册。可是，它的威严尚在，气势尚存。

兴城古城马道

A Ramp of the City Wall in Xingcheng

不知谁说过：建筑是有形的画。从这个意义上讲，这幅立体的城墙之作，不单单是我们的物质文化遗产，更是我们的精神家园。它记录的是坚强不屈的民族精神！

兴城古城魁星楼

兴城古城城墙东南角有一座魁星楼。楼两层，八面八角。内有魁星像一尊，头部像鬼，青脸红发，一脚向后翘起，一手捧斗，一手执笔，犹如用笔点中应试人的姓名，就是古书中说的“魁星点状元”。

精巧的建筑，敬奉着魁星点斗，寄托着人们对文运的期盼，对美好生活的追求。

The Kuixing Pavilion in Xingcheng

Inside the pavilion, a red-haired, blue-faced, ghostly-looking idol of Kuixing (a character in Chinese legend) stands on one leg, holding a brush pen in one hand and a book box in the other, exactly as described in ancient Chinese books when he points out the "Zhuangyuan" (Number One Scholar, the title given to one who scores highest in the imperial examination).

兴城古城钟鼓楼

钟鼓楼居于兴城古城正中。楼高 17.2 米，分为三层。基座平面为正方形，高如城墙，下砌通向四条大街的十字券洞，全部大青砖砌成。上为两层楼阁。周围廊式，歇山卷棚，飞檐凌空，朱廊画栋。西北开涵洞小门，有石阶可上下。

登上钟鼓楼，耳畔响起那悠远的晨钟暮鼓，古城风光尽收眼底，令人心旷神怡。

The Bell Tower in Xingcheng

The Bell Tower of Xingcheng is in the centre of the town. This three-storied building is built solely with dark-grey bricks. It is 17.2 metres high. The top two stories are pavilions and accessible via the stone stairways.

文庙

兴城文庙，亦称孔庙，为旧时祭孔之所。它位于兴城古城内东南隅，始建于明宣德五年（1430年），面积16800平方米，是东北三省最古老的、辽宁省境内最大的一座文庙，为研究明清建筑和儒学活动提供了宝贵资料，是全国重点文物保护单位。

文庙为三进院建筑，东西垣墙南端各有角门一座，东曰毓粹门，西称观德门。第一进院院南为照壁，与南垣墙连立；院北有棂星门，与两侧的圆月门相接。圆月门旁建有碑亭，亭内共立碑碣六幢。过圆月门，便是第二进院。院中泮桥（状元桥）纵跨，桥头有戟门立于高台之上。庭院两侧配以更衣亭、祭品亭、乡贤祠和名宦祠，显得分外雅致。院内古柏参天，曲径通幽。整个建筑群结构严谨，布局合理。照壁、棂星门、泮桥、戟门、大成殿、崇圣寺等主要建筑布局在整个建筑中轴线上。东西两角各有一块石碑，上刻“文武官员军民人等至此下马”。这就是从古至今的下马碑，彰显出孔子这位“至圣先师”的威严。

The Confucius Temple (Wenmiao)

The Confucius Temple, built in 1430, is the place where people worshipped Confucius. Situated in the southeast corner of the town, the temple occupies an area of 16,800 square metres. It is the oldest Confucius temple in Northeast China and the biggest such temple in Liaoning Province.

文庙圆洞门上的砖雕图案

Brick Carvings on the Arch of the Confucius Temple

牡丹似一朵盛开的太阳，芬芳引来双凤翩翩起舞。吉祥，幸福，安详，愉悦……每一种元素都被匠人精心雕刻，在文庙的殿宇间闪烁夺目的光芒。

从棂星门旁的门洞望第二进院

过圆月门，是第二进院。

View of the Second Courtyard from the Arch Beside the Lingxing Arch

圆圆的门，幽幽的径，总想进里看究竟。仄仄的石，绿绿的树，总有世外桃园梦。

兴城文庙棂星门

文庙第一进院内北侧的棂星门，为四柱三间三楼式多房斗拱的木结构牌坊。额上有“棂星门”三个大字，蓝底金字，笔力雄劲，文庙特色跃然而出。棂星门两侧配圆月门，左右两侧各筑碑亭一座，各亭原立碑碣三幢。

The Lingxing Arch of the Confucius Temple in Xingcheng

Lingxing Arch is on the north side of the first courtyard of Confucius Temple. This is a wooden structure with four posts, three spans, three stories and multiple capitals. There is a moon-shaped gate and a stele pavilion on each side of the arch. Each of the pavilions originally housed three steles.

棂星门走过一代又一代秀才、学子，在崇圣祠里祈祷夙愿成为现实——高举高中，光宗耀祖。

文庙第二进院的状元桥

院心有状元桥一座，拱架于池水之上，下有拱形桥孔。桥两侧有汉白玉雕栏，造型优美，做工精细，引人入胜。桥偏北侧原有独立花墙跨院，两院内各建坐北朝南的祠堂三楹，东为乡贤祠，西为名宦祠。桥后庭院正中有戟门立于高台之上。院内南端有东西厢房，分别是更衣亭、祭器库。

石桥，庙宇，树木，甬路……静谧安详，永远是画家心灵追逐的主题。

The Zhuangyuan Bridge in the Second Courtyard of the Confucius Temple

In the centre of the yard, the Zhuangyuan Bridge stands over the pond. Moon arch and white marble carved railings are features of the bridge.

文庙的古松

Old Pine Tree in the Temple

也许是孔圣人的思想感染了文庙的松树。数百春秋寒暑，茂盛如墨，身姿遒劲，注目大地，俯视苍生，看沧海桑田的变迁，看人间冷暖的更替。

卧桐成林

一棵有着几百年历史的梧桐树被台风刮断后，次年在老树干上竟生长出数十棵小桐。几年时间内居然神奇般地长出了一片树林，成为兴城文庙的奇特景观。

A Forest from One Plane Tree

This remarkable view of a forest of young plane trees that has grown out from the fallen trunk of an old plane tree is unique to the temple. The several hundred-year-old plane tree was brought down by a strong wind and amazingly "gave birth" to a few dozen baby plane trees the next year.

林中的每片叶子都是圣人的一片希望。尽管少了山野之气，却依然生机盎然，勃发向上。在这鲜为人知处，独自展示自己的美丽。

大成殿

文庙大成殿，殿中供奉着孔子神位，两侧有四配（颜渊、曾子、孟子、子思）十二哲。门额高悬康熙年间刻制的“万世师表”巨匾一块。大成殿两侧配有东庑和西庑，里面供奉先贤79位，先儒63位。

The Dacheng Hall

Inside the Dacheng Hall, Confucius' altar is in the middle, beside which are statues of his 4 leading disciples and 12 famous students. Along each side walls, there are rows of shrines where idols of 79 sages and 63 scholars are consecrated.

两千年前的崇拜浓缩在一个明代建筑群里。六百年的辉煌闪耀在人杰地灵的宁远城。

祖大乐的石牌坊（从北望去）

祖氏石坊是明末为守卫辽西将领祖大寿、祖大乐兄弟卫明抗清之功而建的旌功坊。现为国家级重点文物。两座牌坊位于兴城古城南街中央，均坐北朝南，相距 85 米。造型皆为仿木结构的四柱三间五楼式。南面的是祖大寿“忠贞胆智”坊，修建于崇祯四年（1631 年），俗称“头道牌楼”。北面的是祖大乐“登坛骏烈”坊，修建于崇祯十一年（1638 年），俗称“二道牌楼”。

View of the Zu Dale Memorial Arch from the North

These Stone Memorial Arches are dedicated to Ming Court Army generals, the brothers Zu Dashou and Zu Dale, for their victory in a battle against Qing forces. Erected in the centre of South Street of Xingcheng 85 metres apart, both of the arches face south and are in the style of wooden structures with four posts, three spans, and five stories.

宁远的山水之间埋葬着多少男儿铮铮铁骨。他们用血肉之躯构铸不朽的长城。而祖氏牌楼，就是这不朽长城上不败的花朵。

祖大寿的石牌坊（从南望去）

祖大寿石坊系用灰白色花岗岩筑造，高约9米，上层额枋刻有“忠贞胆智”、“廓清之烈”，枋间雕刻双龙戏珠和以骑马戎装出征为主题的精美浮雕。祖大乐石坊用赭色岩石筑造，高约12米，上层额枋刻有“登坛骏烈”、“元勋初锡”。枋间浮雕花卉、鸟兽等图案。祖大乐石坊与祖大寿石坊相比较，形制大体相同，只是柱高楼小，更显得巍峨壮观。

View of the Zu Dashou Memorial Arches from the South

The exquisite stone carvings and the impeccable structure of the arches added high artistic value to their historical significance.

祖氏石坊，宁远古城一道靓丽的风景。它代表着明末清初的一段历史；代表着祖氏一门为民族战争而献身沙场的功绩。看着石坊巍峨的身躯，感怀历史的同时，我们也由衷地赞叹古人的智慧与高超的工艺。

祖大乐石牌坊下的石狮子

祖大乐石牌坊下有石头狮子，分立于牌坊中间两柱的南北两侧。兴城人有“摸狮子讨吉祥”的风俗，每到正月十五，延辉街人流汹涌，十数万人争相摸狮子，相当壮观，成为古城一道独特的风景。

Stone Lions under the Zu Dale Arch

面目狰狞，气度不凡。千百年，总是威武不屈，不弃不倦，保一方吉祥安宁。

前所古城

城墙采用大石条砌基，外包青砖，内填黄土夯实。城墙高 3.27 米，宽 6.54 米，周长 2024 米。设城门三座，东门定远，西门永望，南门广定。北城墙正中镶有石匾“中前所”。城墙四角突出，筑有方台。城内还留有药王庙、城隍庙、财神庙等遗迹。

The Historic Town of Qiansuo

The foundation of the wall is built with large stone blocks. The wall was 3.27 metres high, 6.54 metres wide and 2024 metres in circumference and is made of grey bricks sandwiched with loess.

所池森森、墙垛悠悠，人们总猜想一个又一个离奇的故事。而秋末时节，不免有些伤感，萧瑟而又苍凉，像是这个所城的本色。

前所古城西门瓮城

原建的瓮城，唯西门尚存，与城同高，瓮圈长40余米。

Wengcheng (Barbican) of the West Gate of Qiansuo

Barbacan of West Gate is the only original barbacan that remains. It's as tall as the Wall and has a perimeter of more than 40 meters.

望着巍峨高耸的城门，仿佛《前所狼烟》的诗句在耳畔铿锵作响：“眺望高台筑小圆，只因备敌设狼烟。”

觉华岛囤粮城遗址

明代的囤粮城，今存遗址，仍清晰可见。城呈矩形，南北长约 500 米，东西宽约 250 米，墙高约 10 米，底宽约 6 米。北墙设一门，通城外港口，为粮秣、器械运输的通道。南墙设二门，便于岛上往来。东、西墙无门，利于防守。城中有粮囤、料堆及守城官兵营房遗迹，还有一条纵贯南北的排水沟。

明军的粮草城被多尔衮复仇的火焰毁于一旦。而今，古城远去，马放南山，空留无限追忆。

The Ruins of Army Supply Town on Juehua Island

This ruin of Army Supple Town of the Ming Dynasty (1368-1644) is still easily recognizable. Traces of construction in the town include granaries, hay piles and barracks and a drainage ditch running from north to south across the town.

绥中长城

The Suizhong Great Wall

绥中县位于葫芦岛市的西南部，是辽西走廊的最西端，西与河北省秦皇岛市的山海关毗邻，北依层峦叠嶂的燕山山脉与建昌县相连，东与兴城市隔六股河相望，南襟云水苍茫的渤海。依山傍水，扼关内外咽喉要道，是历代兵家必争之地。

明代，这里分属辽东都司的广宁前屯卫和北平都司的永平山海卫、抚宁卫。为防止蒙古鞑靼部、瓦剌部和兀良哈三卫及女真人的侵扰，洪武十四年（1381 年）、正统七年（1442 年）分别在这里修筑蓟镇长城和辽东镇长城。辽东镇长城西端起点与蓟镇长城在锥子山交汇。长城的分布、建筑结构和形制呈多种类型，各种军事防御设施齐全，形成了完备的军事防御体系，充分体现了我国古代军事城防的战略思想，同时也说明了长城建筑“点线结合”的特点。绥中县境内的明代长城是葫芦岛市乃至辽宁省明代长城的重点地区。

Suizhong County is in the southwest of Huludao and at the west end of the Western Liaoning Corridor, with the Shanhaiguan Pass of Qinhuangdao City as its west neighbor, adjoining with Jianchang County and against Yanshan Mountains on the north, opposite Xingcheng City across the Liugu River to the east, and the vast sea of Bohai to its south. This location between mountains and sea makes Suizhong County a strategic natural fort which has been fought over throughout history.

绥中长城各段落名称示意图

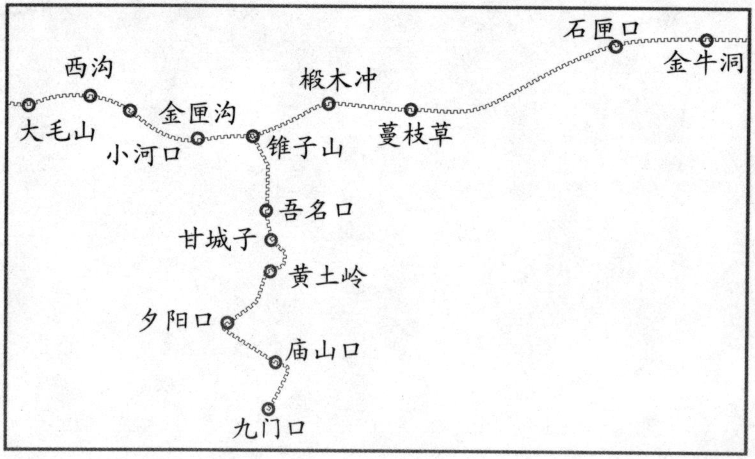

The Plan of the Suizhong Great Wall

The Suizhong Great Wall consists of Liaodong and Jizhen sections. The former section runs 103.2 km from northeast to southwest through 10 towns and 36 villages while the latter stretches 28.6 km through 3 towns and 8 villages.

绥中县明代长城分辽东镇长城和蓟镇长城。

辽东镇长城东北至西南横跨10个乡（镇），36个行政村，全长103.2公里（含副线长城、消失长城）。分为几段，分别为金牛洞、石匣口、蔓枝草、椴木冲、锥子山长城。辽东镇长城的墙体、敌台、烽火台、卫城、所城、堡城、隘口等军事防御工事类型多样化，构成完备的军事防御体系，充分体现了明代长城“点线结合”的构筑特点。其重点防御地域，如山谷、河流两岸和距卫、所、堡城较近的地段，修筑多达三道的长城副线，从而形成纵横交错的防御体系。

蓟镇长城跨3个乡，8个行政村。南起九门口，向北经庙山口、夕阳口、黄土岭、甘城子、吾名口，经锥子山向西，经金匣沟、小河口、西沟、大毛山等段长城，全长28.6公里。蓟镇长城区别于辽东镇长城之处，在于其墙体高而宽，在重点地段如关隘，多修筑高大砖墙，地势险要或不重要地段多筑石墙，而且山险多人工铲削。另外，敌台、马面、烽火台，星罗棋布。

绥中县的长城，选择修筑在崇山峻岭之中，就成为“天险”，如锥子山长城、石匣口长城等；因河而筑，就构成“固塞”，如狗河、石河沿岸分布的长城；或者利用险山，不筑墙垣，只是在山口险要处设有关隘——因山为塞，集中体现了“因地制宜，就地取材”和“因山边险，因河为固”的建筑特点。

九门口长城（一）

位于李家堡乡新堡子村，为世界文化遗产。现存砖墙约 2300 米，以自然山体为基础，墙基采用条石错缝垒砌，墙体用青砖砌筑，宽 3.5 ～ 6 米，高 8 米。

九江河有石铺的河底，九江河有砖筑的城桥，“城在水上走，水在城中流”。

The Jiumenkou Great Wall (1)

The Jiumenkou Great Wall is in Xinpuzi Village of Lijiapu Town. The 2300-metre wall is built on top of the hill, the foundation laid with stone blocks and the body of the wall made of grey bricks. The wall is 8 metres high and 3.5 to 6 metres wide.

九门口长城（二）

九门口长城是由城墙、敌楼、马面、边台、围城、过河城桥、关城、哨楼、拦马沟、拦马墙、烽火台、炮台等一系列军事防御工事以及其他附属设施构成，是我国目前独一无二的水上长城。它号称“京东首关”，是山海关及京东防御体系的羽翼，是保卫山海关及京师的重要屏障。

The Jiumenkou Great Wall (2)

The only section of The Great Wall built in the water.

古老的御敌城墙架在河床之上，且有九门为关。人们感慨它的神奇，更赞美古人的智慧。千百年啦，流水匆匆，岁月茫茫，而这道雄关依然岿然不动。

九门口闸门

九门口水上长城的护城拱门，一共九个，并排横贯在峡谷间，固若金汤。

The Jiumenkou Lock Gate

The Jiumenkou water gate on the Great Wall has nine arches, spans the canyon from side to side, an impregnable barrier.

庙山口长城

图中的敌台是庙山口段长城 3 号敌台，墙体是石结构的墙体，毛石包砌，白灰勾缝。

The Miaoshankou Great Wall

The lookout tower in the picture is No. 3 watchtower of the Miaoshankou Great Wall. The wall is made of stone with white lime mortar.

高耸云端的敌楼，也是智慧的顶点。且战且防且住且宿——城堡的功能，固体的景观，成为长城永恒的标志。

夕阳口长城

位于李家堡乡娄家沟村。现存砖墙约 2600 米，以自然山体为基础，墙基采用条石错缝垒砌，墙体用青砖和大块毛石砌筑；现存墙体宽 3.5 ～ 6 米，高 3.5 ～ 8 米。

一座山峰，一朵敌台。狼烟已远，炮声不再，空余旧迹任时间安排——而时空不会再现“一夫当关，万夫莫开”的景象。

The Xiyangkou Great Wall

The Xiyangkou Great Wall is located at Loujiagou village, Lijiapu Town. The existing brick wall was based on natural mountain and extends about 2600 meters. The base of the wall was built with stone slabs and the wall body is made of grey bricks and large stones. The width of the wall is 3.5 to 6 meters and the height is 3.5 to 8 meters.

夕阳口长城残破的敌台

墙体为石结构，用毛石包砌至顶，白灰勾缝，中间用毛石填充，顶部外侧为石砌垛口墙，内侧不设女墙。

一道壁立的墙，一块不倒的碑，在大地的高耸处，在丛林的更深处——默默无闻，我行我素。

Ruined Watchtower of the Xiyangkou Great Wall

This part of wall was built of stones. The outside of the top has crenellations, but there is no parapet wall inside.

黄土岭长城

黄土岭关是蓟镇长城的重要关隘之一，黄土岭长城三段石墙是蓟镇长城的重要段落之一，其建筑形式与蓟镇石筑长城相同。

The Huangtuling Great Wall

The Huangtuling Pass was one of the key passes of the Jizhen Great Wall.The third section shown here is one of the important parts of the Jizhen Great Wall. It has the same design as Jizhen stone Great Wall.

一楼更比一楼高，高楼却在天尽头。从东至西，洋洋万里，城墙连接多少这样的敌楼。

甘城子长城

甘城子长城第7段石墙。蓟镇长城的段落之一，该段石墙的建筑形式与蓟镇其他石筑长城相同。

The Ganchengzi Great Wall

The stone wall of the seventh section of the Ganchengzi Great Wall is one of the important parts of Jizhen Great Wall. The architectural style of this stone wall is the same as other stone walls of Jizhen Great Wall.

碎石残砖颓败的城墙，尽管遗迹空留，目不忍睹，可气势不倒，精神永驻。

吾名口关关门

吾名口关是蓟镇长城南段的重要关隘。位于李家堡乡锥山沟村。现存砖墙 2450 米，墙体以自然山体为基础，墙基采用条石错缝垒砌，墙体用青砖和大块毛石砌筑；现存墙体宽 3.5 ～ 6 米，高 3.5 ～ 7 米。从涵洞中看见的是锥子山的山体。

The Wumingkou Pass

The Wumingkou Pass is located in Zhuishangou Village of Lijiapu Town. The 2450-metre wall is built on top of the hill, the foundation laid with stone blocks and the body of the wall made of grey bricks and large stones. The wall is 3.5 to 6 metres high and 3.5 to 7 metres wide. What we see through the arch is Zhuizi Mountain.

城墙的涵洞，像探窥历史的眼睛——里面有模糊的风景，充满吾名口的深秋。

蓟镇长城南线

South Stretch of the Jizhen Great Wall

此处点狼烟，彼处举烽火，用原始的方式传递着消息，互相携手抗击来犯之敌。

锥子山以南蓟镇长城

The Jizhen Great Wall to the South of Zhuizi Mountain

时间就是历史。不知何时，不知是风是鸟把种子播下，平展的敌楼上长满了青松，远山依旧，长城悠悠。

金匣沟长城

锥子山西侧长城墙体为砖石结构，条石基础，其上砌青砖至顶，墙体上部外侧为垛口墙，内侧为女墙。敌台为二层空心，砖石结构，条石基础，其上砌青砖至顶，其台体内部为三个卷棚式券室，并在台体两侧各设一门，台体四周设有箭窗，靠其券室一侧设有可登至顶部的楼梯；台体顶部四周为垛口墙，设有瞭望孔、射孔，顶部设有铺舍，其建筑形式为硬山式仿木结构。

忽然，有一个想象：山是长城的根基；长城是山的通道；而敌楼就是这通道上的驿站。

The Jinxiagou Great Wall

The walls at the west end of the Zhuizishan Great Wall are brick and stone constructions. The outer wall has crenellations, and the inner wall has a parapet wall. The watchtower is a two-storey, hollow-interior construction.

敌楼

A Watchtower of the Great Wall

敌台是长城的骨节，连结的不止是一段和另一段城墙，更是通讯给养的平台。星罗的敌台，不知演绎了多少神秘的故事。

小河口长城第2段砖墙

该段墙体为砖结构，其基础为条石，其上全部是青砖砌筑，墙体上部外侧为垛口墙，内侧为女墙。在垛口墙设有瞭望孔与射孔。

The Second Segment of the Xiaohekou Great Wall

This section of wall is made of bricks with a stone foundation. The outer wall has watch holes and crenellations and the inner wall is a parapet.

千百年的工事，像个不朽的崇拜。蕴天地灵气，汲万世营养。长城——你一身龙骨，你横跃千山万壑，腾空而起；你气势吞宇，傲视苍穹；你开天辟地，亘古奇迹。

小河口长城第6段砖石结构的墙体

位于永安堡乡西沟村。现存砖墙约2100米，以自然山体为基础，墙基采用条石错缝垒砌，墙体用青砖和大块毛石砌筑；现存墙体宽2.5～6米，高1.5～6米。

The Sixth Segment of the Xiaohekou Great Wall Features Brick and Stone Masonry Structure

This watchtower is located in Xigou Village of Yong'anpu Town. The remaining 2100 metres wall is built on top of the mountain rocks and the foundation laid with overlapping stone blocks, the body of the wall made of grey bricks and large stones. What remains of the wall is 1.5 to 6 metres high and 2.5 to 6 metres wide.

西沟长城

位于永安堡乡西沟村。现存砖墙2250米，以自然山体为基础，墙基采用条石错缝垒砌，白灰勾缝，墙体用青砖和大块毛石砌筑；现存墙体宽2.5～6米，高3.5～8米。

The Xigou Great Wall

The Xigou Great Wall is located in Xigou Village of Yong'anpu Town. The remaining brick wall is 2250 metres long. It is built on top of the mountain rocks, the foundation was laid with overlapping stone blocks and lime mortar and the body of the wall is made of grey bricks and large stones. The remaining wall is 3.5 to 8 metres high and 2.5 to 6 metres wide.

一阶叠一阶的墙垣，一山高过一山的敌楼，把思绪带向更高的境界。凝重的气象，夸张的手法，画家的心和戚继光的心脉脉相通。一个在画纸上涂抹写意，一个在大地上描绘宏图……

西沟长城敌楼

Watchtower at the Xigou Great Wall

一块残缺的无字碑，一幅完美的写意画。在冬日的阳光下，显得更加雄壮。这是古人馈赠的财富；这是古人留存的纪念。

大毛山长城

大毛山口是西沟长城线上的一个重要隘口。据说，大毛山口的诨名是因为在山岭下的南面有一小山头，其状如蹲踞的猫，面对着岭上的隘口，故称此山口为“大猫山口”，后来人们叫白了，称之为“大毛山口”。

The Damaoshan Great Wall

Damaoshan Pass is an important pass along the Xigou Great Wall. It is said that to the south of the foot of the mountain there was a small hill that looked like a crouching cat facing the mountain pass and that's why it was named Big Cat ("Damao") Pass. Later it was called Damaoshan Pass because of the similar and easier pronunciation in Chinese.

依天险地势，造人文关隘。城墙倚山高，目光需仰止。是守卫与战争的需要，用智慧发明了长城；是历史与现实的节点，用审美光大了长城。

大毛山长城残破的敌台

残破的敌台耸立在松涛云海之中。

Ruined Watchtower at the Damaoshan Great Wall

The dilapidated watchtower looms above the pine forest and the sea of clouds.

城墙的每一个垛口都是警觉的前哨。看那黝黑的射洞和狰狞的礌石口，捍卫着明王朝的威严与神圣。

锥子山长城（一）

位于永安堡乡花户庄村。现存石墙 1928 米，山险 560 米。其中，石墙以自然山体为基础，用大块毛石错缝垒砌，白灰勾缝，中间填充碎石，墙体顶部用毛石垒砌垛口墙；现存墙体宽 1.5 ～ 4.3 米，高 1.25 ～ 9.8 米。

The Zhuizishan Great Wall (1)

The Zhuizishan Great Wall is located in Huahuzhuang Village of Yong'anpu Town. The remaining stone wall is 1928 metres long while the mountain forms a natural barrier 560 metres in length. A stone wall is built on top of the mountain rocks. When building the stone walls, gravel is sandwiched between lime-mortared overlapping large stones. The remaining wall is 1.25 to 9.8 metres high and 1.5 to 4.3 metres wide.

山是立体的、墙是立体的、楼是立体的。不想用险峻之类的词汇赞美你；不想用伟大之类的词汇描绘你——而你，是中国真正的巨龙，真正的图腾！千百年来，一直生动在每一个人的心里。

锥子山长城（二）

锥子山既是辽东镇长城与蓟镇长城的分界线，又是两镇长城的交汇点。从图中可看到，长城都没有修到锥子山山顶，因山险本身就可以防御敌军侵入。

The Zhuizishan Great Wall (2)

The Zhuizishan Great Wall is both the dividing line and the meeting place of the Liaodong and Jizhen Great Wall. Making use of the natural barrier of the mountain, neither of the two sections has been built to the mountain top, which can be seen in the picture.

椴木冲长城

位于永安堡乡大甸子村。现存石墙 1407 米，山险约 1600 米。其中，石墙以自然山体为基础，两侧用大块毛石错缝垒砌，白灰勾缝，中间填充碎石；现存墙体宽 2.3 ～ 7.4 米，高 2.2 ～ 6.7 米。

The Duanmuchong Great Wall

The Duanmuchong Great Wall is located in Dadianzi Village of Yong'anpu Town. The remaining stone wall is 1407 metres long while the mountain forms 1600 metres of natural barrier. A stone wall is built on top of the mountain rocks. The remaining wall is 2.2 to 6.7 metres high and 2.3 to 7.4 metres wide.

这不仅仅是一蠡城楼，更是历史的横断层。它标志着一个画地为牢、戍边成墙的时代成为历史；也说明一个现代文明对古老遗存的包容与偏爱。

蔓枝草长城

位于永安堡乡大甸子村。现存石墙1638米，山险423米。其中，石墙以自然山体为基础，用较规整的大块毛石错缝垒砌，外部白灰勾缝，内部以碎石填充，墙顶海墁用片石铺砌；现存墙体宽2～7.3米，高0.8～6米。

岁月的刻痕不减，老去了容颜，不老的江山。

The Manzhicao Great Wall

The Manzhicao Great Wall is located in Dadianzi Village of Yong'anpu Town. The remaining stone wall is 1638 metres long while the mountain forms 423 metres of natural barrier. A stone wall is built on top of the mountain rocks. In building the stone walls, gravel is sandwiched between lime-mortared overlapping large stones. The remaining wall is 0.8 to 6 metres high and 2 to 7.3 metres wide.

金牛洞长城

位于永安堡乡獐狼铳村。现存石墙 489 米，山险 1200 米。其中，石墙依山势砌筑在基岩上，用较规整的大块毛石错缝垒砌，白灰勾缝，中间填充碎石，顶部外侧砌有垛口墙，部分段落砌有女墙；现存墙体宽 6.4 ～ 7.6 米，高 0.2 ～ 6.2 米。

The Jinniudong Great Wall

The Jinniudong Great Wall is located in Zhanglangtong Village of Yong'anpu Town. The remaining stone wall is 489 metres long while the mountain forms 1200 metres of natural barrier. A stone wall is built on top of the mountain rocks. In building the stone walls, gravel is sandwiched between lime-mortared overlapping large stones. The outer wall on top has crenellations and the inner wall is parapet. The remaining wall is 0.2 to 6.2 metres high and 6.4 to 7.6 metres wide.

一座座敌楼、一颗颗珍珠，点缀在莽莽苍苍的北国。上千年啦，依然是凝固的风景。

锥子山长城东段

该段长城墙体为毛石结构，以山体岩石为基础，墙体两侧用大块规整毛石包砌，白灰勾缝，中间用大小不一的毛石填充，墙体顶部利用山势走向砌筑成阶梯式的建筑形式，墙体两侧用石头砌筑垛口墙与女墙。其敌台为二层空心、回字形的建筑方式，砖石结构，条石基础，其上砌青砖至顶，其内部结构是四周为回廊，中间设一大券室，在其一侧设有登至顶部的楼梯。台体顶部四周为垛口墙，设有瞭望孔、射孔，顶部设有铺舍，现存基础。

沿着蜿蜒的山脊，一阶又一阶筑就。坚不可摧的城防，阻挡了外来之敌，却也禁固了中原飞翔的翅膀。

The East Section of the Zhuizishan Great Wall

This stone wall is part of the Liaodongzhen Great Wall to the East of Zhuizishan. Only the foundation remains.

三台子烽火台

戚继光于明隆庆四年（1570 年）主持修筑，是绥中境内保存比较完好的一座明代烽火台，形体高大。该烽火台属路台，平面呈圆形，通高 15 米。条石砌基，台身用青砖砌筑，正面设有弓形券门，台顶留有垛口，并建有长方形的铺房及烽火灶。

Santaizi Beacon Tower

This well-preserved large and tall Beacon Tower in Suizhong was built in 1570 supervised by the famous Ming general Qi Jiguang.

这不仅仅是一个砖砌的土台，还是完备御敌体系的关键点。当狼烟冲天报告一个个军讯，来犯之敌就有可能葬身城墙之侧。

夕阳口长城1号烽火台

该台平面呈矩形，以山体岩石为基础，台体用不规则的毛石砌筑，建于长城主体内侧的高阜之处。其用途是当发现敌情时报警，白天举烟，夜晚举火，故名烽火台。

堆砌的峰，矗立的台，兀立的树，像胜利者鲜艳的旗帜，在高高的山巅飘扬。

No. 1 Beacon Tower of the Xiyangkou Great Wall

This tower has a trapezoid plan, and is built on the hill body with irregular shaped stones. It is used to send out alarm signals—smoke during the daytime and fire at night.

敌台的墙体

敌台的墙体用规整的大块毛石错缝垒砌。经过数百年的时间，仍完好如初。

The Walls of a Watchtower

The walls of the watchtower were all laid with large overlapping stones which remain intact, as they were hundreds of years ago.

拱门空悠，城墙突兀，绿树疯长着蓬勃生机，而故事早已成为一个又一个传说。

小河口长城4号敌台

该敌台坐落在小河口屯西南方向的长城墙体上，平面呈矩形。二层空心，由于早年遭到破坏，现已残破不堪，只留下残垣断壁。其用途一是作为守卫长城的单体防御工事，二是作为官兵食宿之所。

No. 4 Watchtower of the Xiaohekou Great Wall

No. 4 Watchtower is located on the section of the Great Wall that runs from south to west in Xiaohekou Village. This two-storey watchtower is rectangular in plan and has a hollow interior. The tower provided shelter for the soldiers and served as a fortress. The tower has been damaged badly and become a ruin.

砖木结构的城墙，葱郁的树木掩映，构成立体的壁画，展示粗犷的美。尽管影子残缺破损，昔日的雄风似乎不再，即便是苍老的躯体，也要保持挺立的姿式。

墙体（一）

小河口长城第 6 段砖石结构的墙体。

The Wall (1)

The brick and stone masonry walls of the 6th segment of the Xiaohekou Great Wall.

残损的垛口一如褴褛的老人，心中装满苦涩的故事，静默地守候着未来时光。

墙体（二）

The Wall (2)

锥子山长城的山险及石墙

The Stone Walls and the Natural Barrier of Zhuizishan Great Wall

在绥中的锥子山上，有着一段段别样的长城。不用砖不用石也不用土垒，以山为险以山为墙。山顶是一座又一座烽火台。这是古人的智慧——一夫当关，万夫莫开！

小河口一段山险

该段是利用其险峻的山体、峭壁，随山势起伏而自然形成的一道天然屏障。

The “Mountain Wall” along the Xiaohekou Great Wall

The steep mountain cliffs have been used as a natural barrier in this section.

这长满长城的江山，广袤厚重，伟大神奇。

鼓山长城山险墙

位于永安堡乡边外村。现存石墙 1435 米，山险墙 587 米，山险 972 米。其中，石墙以自然山体为基础，大块毛石错缝垒砌，白灰勾缝，中间填充碎石；现存墙体宽 2.4 ～ 7.2 米，高 0.4 ～ 5.5 米。山险墙是利用山体自然陡峭的脊部进行人工铲削或稍加整理而形成的墙体，有的在山脊平缓处修筑低矮石墙。

大山是阴森的屏障，敌楼就是睁着的眼睛，时时注视来犯之敌——神圣的使命从来不敢淡忘。

The “Mountain Wall” of Gushan

The Gushan Great Wall is located in Bianwai Village of Yong’anpu Town. There remains 1435 metres of stone wall, another 587 metres of natural barrier and 972 metres of low wall built atop steep cliffs. In the walls, gravel is sandwiched between lime-mortared overlapping large stones. The remaining wall is 0.4 to 5.5 metres high and 2.4 to 7.2 metres wide.

历史脉络

Veins of History

葫芦岛市刚刚建市 20 多年（原名锦西，1994 年 10 月更名），是个年轻的城市。它地处辽西丘陵，有几条东北—西南走向的山脉，群山中有几条河流，东南沿海为狭长的平原。北靠松岭，南临渤海，是著名的辽西走廊，古往今来的兵家必争之地。

六千年来，人类从蒙昧走向文明。这个过程伴随着杀伐、吞并、迁徙、逃奔。辽西走廊地带六千年是一部不同文化交流、碰撞与冲突的历史。

新石器时期，南票区沙锅屯有上古人的遗址。战国时期，中原汉民族就对辽西进行过文化开发。秦皇汉武、魏主曹操都在辽西留下过深深的脚印。东汉末年，北方游牧民族南进。隋唐至五代，汉民族恢复了对辽西走廊的控制权。隋唐九征高丽，强化了不同民族的交融。10 世纪往后的 400 年，先有契丹人进入，后有女真人和蒙古人占据。一次次游牧民族南进，也是一次次重要的民族融合。明清时期是古代中国民族的最后一次大融合。明朝由于边防的需要，辽西文化进入大发展。清朝满、汉、蒙古、回、朝鲜、锡伯等民族共同生息在这块土地上。九一八事变爆发，辽西十四年沦陷。辽西人民和全国人民一样，救亡图存，付出巨大牺牲，终于迎来中华民族的解放。抗战胜利后的 1946 年，在葫芦岛港，遣返百万日侨俘，用一个民族的宽仁和爱心，去温暖这个明清以来不断送来灾祸和血腥的近邻。解放战争，塔山阻击战，在国家“两种前途、两种命运”的抉择中，辽西人民用汗水、鲜血和生命，使一个民族的命运从此彻底转变。

阅过走廊地带六千年历史，就会发现，葫芦岛及其周边地区的文化史，是一部见证中国民族性格和魅力的历史。

Huludao City is a young city only 20 years old. Rivers runs through the mountain ranges, and a strip of plain stretches along the southeast coast line. Looking south towards the Bohai Bay and nestling against the Songling Mountains to its north, the city is also part of the Western Liaoning Corridor, a piece of land that was always a strategic military hotspot.

沙锅屯洞穴遗址

沙锅屯洞穴遗址位于葫芦岛市南票区沙锅屯乡媳妇山东坡天然洞穴中。山洞洞口高约2米，宽约3米，深近10米。洞内自然形成三部分空间，向里逐渐缩小，略呈牛角形。该遗址1921年6月由应中国政府之聘来华做地质调查的瑞典地质学家安特生博士发现。遗址中出土了很多石器、骨器、陶片和45具人骨，属红山文化类型。沙锅屯遗址是近代田野考古技术引入中国的第一个正式发掘地，在中国考古学史上具有里程碑意义。

七千年前的塞外并不荒凉，我们祖先已斧凿火煮在山洞中。石斧彩陶和仰韶文化同根同源。古人的骨殖虽然已被国外馆藏，而洞穴的价值却不是语言所能表述。

The Shaguotun Cave Site

The Shaguotun Cave is a natural cave on the East slope of the Xifu Mountain in Shaguotun, Nanpiao district of Huludao City. The cave is 2 metres high, 3 metres wide and 10 metres deep. There are three natural sections of the cave. The cave narrows down as it gets deeper, forming a funnel shape. It was discovered by Swedish geologist Dr. Andersson (Johan Gunnar Andersson) in June 1921 while conducting a geological survey at the invitation of the Chinese government. Numerous stone and bone tools, pottery pieces, and 45 human skeletons were found in the cave, which were identified as from the prehistoric Hongshan Culture.

绥中碣石宫（秦汉）遗址

1982年春天发现于万家镇，是我国发掘的最早的古代建筑群之一。遗迹分六处，分布在南北长4公里、东西长3.5公里的海滩上。类似于咸阳宫的建制与布局，排水沟道、贮藏窖井、房屋基础在遗迹中清晰可见。遗迹的中轴线恰好正对着海中的巨石。

The Suizhong Site of the Jieshi Palace (Qin and Han Dynasty)

Located in Wanjia Town, this is one of the first excavations in China of a group of ancient buildings. The extensive Qin and Han Palace ruins were discovered in 1982. The ruins are in six groups located on a stretch of beach in an area that is 4 km from north to south and 3.5 km from east to west. The plan of the ruins is similar to that of Xianyang Palace (near Xi'an).

这不是秦始皇行宫上的瓦当吗？刀叉剑戟依稀是战场的缩影。惊涛拍岸，气宇轩昂，彰显一代英雄成就霸业后的豪气。

寻觅碣石宫

在绥中止锚湾海滨，距海岸200多米的海水中屹立着三块不规则的巨石，民间传说那是孟姜女投海自尽的地方，称之为姜女石。偶然遇到落大潮的时候，隐约可见海水中有一条石条铺成的路从海岸通向巨石。

三块巨石，传说有一块曾搭在两尊石柱之上，那是茫茫渤海耸起的古国之门。

The Legend of Jieshi Palace

On the beach of Suizhong Maowan Bay, 200 metres away from the coast stand three large rocks, called Jiangnü Rocks. Legend has it that this is where Meng Jiangnü jumped into the sea and killed herself. At low tide, there is the illusion of a path leading to the rock in the sea.

前卫斜塔

位于绥中县前卫镇。建于辽代，又名瑞州古塔。现存塔身高10米，塔身向东北方向倾斜8度，塔尖水平位移1米多。该塔建成之后虽几经地震与洪水破坏，却始终斜而不倒。

The Qianwei Leaning Pagoda

The Qianwei Leaning Pagoda (Ruizhou Ancient Pagoda) is situated in Qianwei Town, Suizhong County and is more than a thousand years old. The body of the pagoda is now 10 metres high, and leaning at an angle towards the Northeast. The top of the pagoda has moved more than one meter away from its original position. This pagoda has experienced several earthquakes and floods, but none of them could bring the pagoda down.

风雨剥蚀千年，还坚强地屹立着，媲美意大利的比萨斜塔。倾斜也是特有神态，一种桑沧的美，一种不颓的美。

沙锅屯石塔

建于金泰和年间，是辽宁省迄今所发现的最早的石塔之一。此塔用褐色花岗岩雕琢砌筑而成，六角密檐式，由基座、塔身、塔檐、塔刹四部分构成。通高 4.6 米，须弥座高 0.95 米，枋上有一厚 20 厘米、直径 50 厘米的石圆盘，盘周雕仰莲。塔身立于圆盘之上，每面正中雕有尖券式佛龛。塔檐间距基本相等，由下而上逐层内收成锥形。

The Shaguotun Stone Pagoda

The Shaguotun Stone Pagoda, the oldest one found in Liaoning Province, is more than a thousand years old. This hexagonal pagoda, built and finely sculptured of brown granite has a roof with many closely-set eaves, a design termed Miyan in Chinese.

在凸起的岩石之上，你像一把锋利的剑，造型独特，神态威武。蕴天地之灵气，积历史之厚重。

兴城白塔峪塔

建于辽大安八年（1092 年），高 43 米，砖筑八角十三级实心密檐式。须弥座的转角处有砖雕天王力士作承托状，塔身八角各嵌有石刻倚柱，刻有八大灵塔的塔名。

The Xingcheng Baitayu Pagoda

The Xingcheng Baitayu Pagoda was built in 1092. It is an octagonal 13 storey pagoda 43 metres high with a solid interior and built in the Miyan style. On the corner of the base (called Xumizuo) the brick carvings depict the God of Strength (Dalishen) who is positioned at the base as if carrying the pagoda. The names of the eight great stupas are engraved on the eight corners of the base.

你虽然远离觉华佛岛，大龙宫寺的殿顶却尽收眼底。为着一代高僧不忘的纪念，千百年还在坚守着忠诚。

妙峰寺双塔

位于绥中县永安堡乡塔子沟村，建于辽乾统年间。两塔之间相距 40 米，东塔高约 24 米，为八角九级实心密檐塔，西塔高约 10 米，为六角五级密檐实心塔。两塔结构基本相同，塔身底层各面均雕有佛像。周围山峦起伏，丛绿滴翠，桑柏如织，景致秀丽。

The Twin Pagodas in Miaofeng Temple

The "twins" are located 40 metres apart in Tazigou Village of Yong'anpu Town, Suizhong County. The one in the east stands 24 metres high, is a nine-storey octagon, with a solid interior and close-set eaves. The one in the west is a 10 metres high, five-storey hexagon also with a solid interior and close-set eaves. They share a similar structure and have carvings of Buddha around the base.

咫尺的距离已是天涯之隔，四十米是不可跨越的天堑。那么就永远这般注视吧，注视对方也注视历史和现实。

水下考古发现的元代瓷器

葫芦岛市绥中县元代沉船遗址，厚 1.1 ～ 3.6 米，最高顶面高于海底 2.5 米。出土的是一艘满载瓷器的商船，其出露海底部分已完全被沉积物所覆盖，非常坚硬。遗址发掘历时 7 年，挖掘了一大批元代完整的瓷器及残片，是我国水下考古队独立完成的第一个考古项目。

Underwater Archeological Discovery: Yuan Dynasty (1206-1368) Porcelain

The excavation of the Yuan Dynasty (1206-1368) shipwreck found in Suizhong County took 7 years. Numerous whole and broken items of porcelain ware found.

偌大的木船沉了，舱里的瓷器坠了，细沙微澜，船体和坛坛罐罐沉睡千年。七年的打捞，俊美的容颜重见天日——天鹅飞翔，莲花童子，江天暮雪。

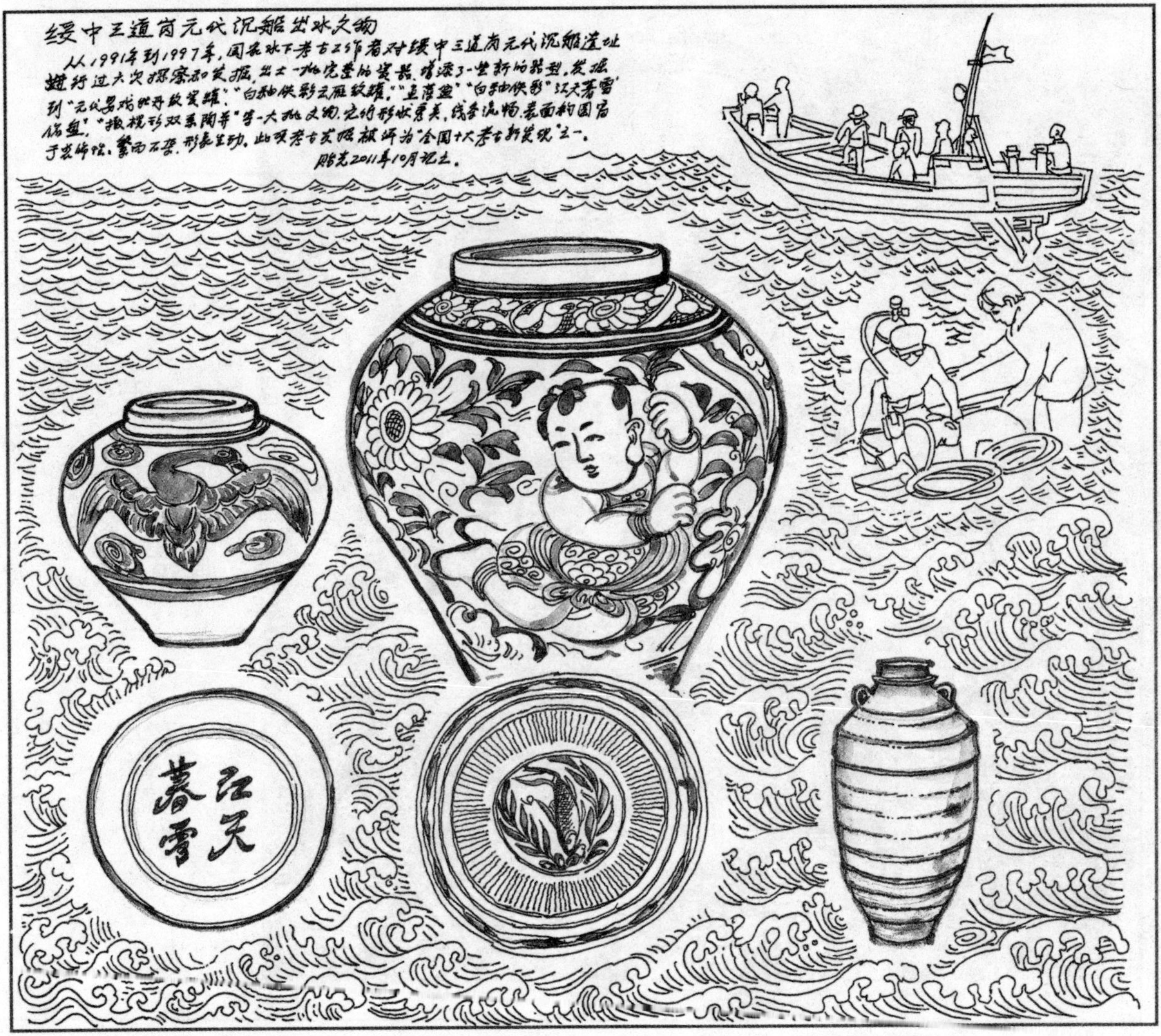

朱梅墓园

墓园中有两座青色花岗岩刻造的高大石坊，四柱三楼式，单檐庑殿顶。立于明崇祯十年（1637年），因朱梅（字海峰）镇守山海关有功御赐。墓前有石狮、石羊、石马、石人各一对，是辽宁省唯一的规模较大、保存较完整的明代石刻群。

Zhu Mei's Tomb

Zhumei's tomb is located in Shipaifang Village of Lijia Town, Suizhong County. It has the only large-scale well-preserved collection of Ming stone carvings in Liaoning Province. In 1637, the emperor bestowed this monument on his highest ranking general Zhu Mei for successfully defending the Shanhaiguan Pass.

高大的石坊是对你最好的表彰。代表着你显赫的戎马生涯，也代表着你不朽的丰功伟绩。

文化的交融

北方游牧文化与中原农耕文化在四百里辽西走廊经过了数百年的交流与融合，在石刻艺术品中，在现存的民居建筑中，都保留着不同文化的元素。

The Intermingling of Cultures

The nomadic, pastoral people of the Northern grasslands, and the people from the Central Plains of China with their farming culture, have intermingled for centuries in the area of the Western Liaoning Corridor. Different cultural elements can be identified in the stone carvings and residential buildings.

卧冰取鱼的汉人王祥盘着契丹族的小辫儿，北方朱梅墓上的雄狮显示出江南石雕的风格，各怀绝技的道教八仙，生龙活虎的契丹民族，南方的一切和北方的所有在这里融合。

葫芦岛大遣返

1946年5月7日，两艘满载着2489名日侨俘的轮船拉开了葫芦岛大遣返的帷幕。在一年多中，共遣返日侨俘158批1051047人。此举规模之大、人员之多、时间之长，实属罕见，反映出中国人民以德报怨的伟大人道主义精神。

The Huludao Repatriation of the Japanese

On May 7, 1946, a ship carrying 2489 Japanese people left Huludao for Japan, the first part of the scheme to repatriate Japanese prisoners and residents from Huludao to their home country. Over a period of just over one year, a total of 1,051,047 Japanese were repatriated in 158 batches.

穿和服的姐姐背着熟睡的弟弟，孤寡的母亲带着年幼的儿女，还有战败后不再耀武扬威的兵丁——中国人民以德报怨提供粮食药品，葫芦岛给了百万日侨俘生的希望。葫芦岛大遣返——一首人道主义精神的伟大赞歌。

塔山阻击战

塔山为沿海丘陵地貌，南临大海，北依虹螺山，是辽西走廊进入关东的最后一处锁钥之地。塔山阻击战是我军阻击增援锦州的国民党军的一次著名战役，对辽沈战役起到了关键作用。纪念塔建成于 1963 年 10 月 15 日，建在战争时的我军前沿指挥所处。塔高 12.5 米。

The Tashan Battle

The winning of Tashan Battle enabled the army to triumph at the Battle of Liao-Shen in the War of Liberation. The battle monument was erected on Oct. 15, 1963 on the spot where the command post was located.

葫芦岛和平宣言

2006 年 6 月，在葫芦岛市隆重举行“葫芦岛百万日侨大遣返 60 周年回顾暨中日关系展望论坛”，在论坛结束时发表了葫芦岛和平宣言：“我们谴责侵略，反对战争。我们以史为鉴，面向未来。我们热切呼吁并郑重宣言：让战争的罪恶远离人类，让和平的阳光永驻人间。”

The Huludao Peace Declaration

In June 2006, a meeting to commemorate the 60th anniversary of repatriation of over one million Japanese migrants from Huludao and Forum on China-Japan Relations was held in Huludao and at the end of the meeting the Huludao Peace Declaration was made.

名胜探幽

Exploration of Historic Sites

地处辽西走廊、辽东湾的葫芦岛市，堪称京东关外第一市、雄鸡项下一明珠。它集山、海、城、泉、岛于一体，山在城中，城在海边，城岛相依。得天独厚的自然条件及悠远的历史，为葫芦岛市留下众多弥足珍贵的风物景观。

Huludao City, located on Liaodong Bay, West Liaoning corridor, truly deserves the title of First City East of Beijing Outside of Shanhaiguan Pass. It boasts of mountains, towns, springs, islands and the sea, with the views of mountains in the city and city beside the sea. The unique natural conditions and the long history of the city have created many precious landscapes in Huludao City.

觉华岛俯瞰

觉华岛原名菊花岛，俗称大海山，由磨盘山岛、张山子岛、杨山子岛等四个岛屿及一双人礁组成。主岛长葫芦形，两头宽阔，中间窄细，斜卧海中。面积13.5平方公里，是辽东湾最大的岛屿。东北至西南走向长6公里，南北宽1至4公里。中间有一细谷，南北长1公里，东西宽0.5公里，将岛分成东西两部分，东大西小。东半部山势险峻，多为悬崖峭壁，最高峰大架山，海拔198.2米。

海天相接，浪盈波涌，夕阳晚归，渔船点点。这蓝色大海中的美丽小岛，风光秀丽，人杰地灵。

Bird's-eye View of Juehua Island

Juehua Island, commonly known as Dahaishan (the Sea Mountain), is the largest group of islands in Liaodong Bay. It consists of Mopanshan Island, Zhangshanzi Island and Yangshanzi Island together with a pair of reefs. The main island is in the shape of a long gourd and covers an area of 13.5 square kilometres. The eastern part of island is decked with cliffs and the peak Dajiashan has an elevation of 198.2 meters.

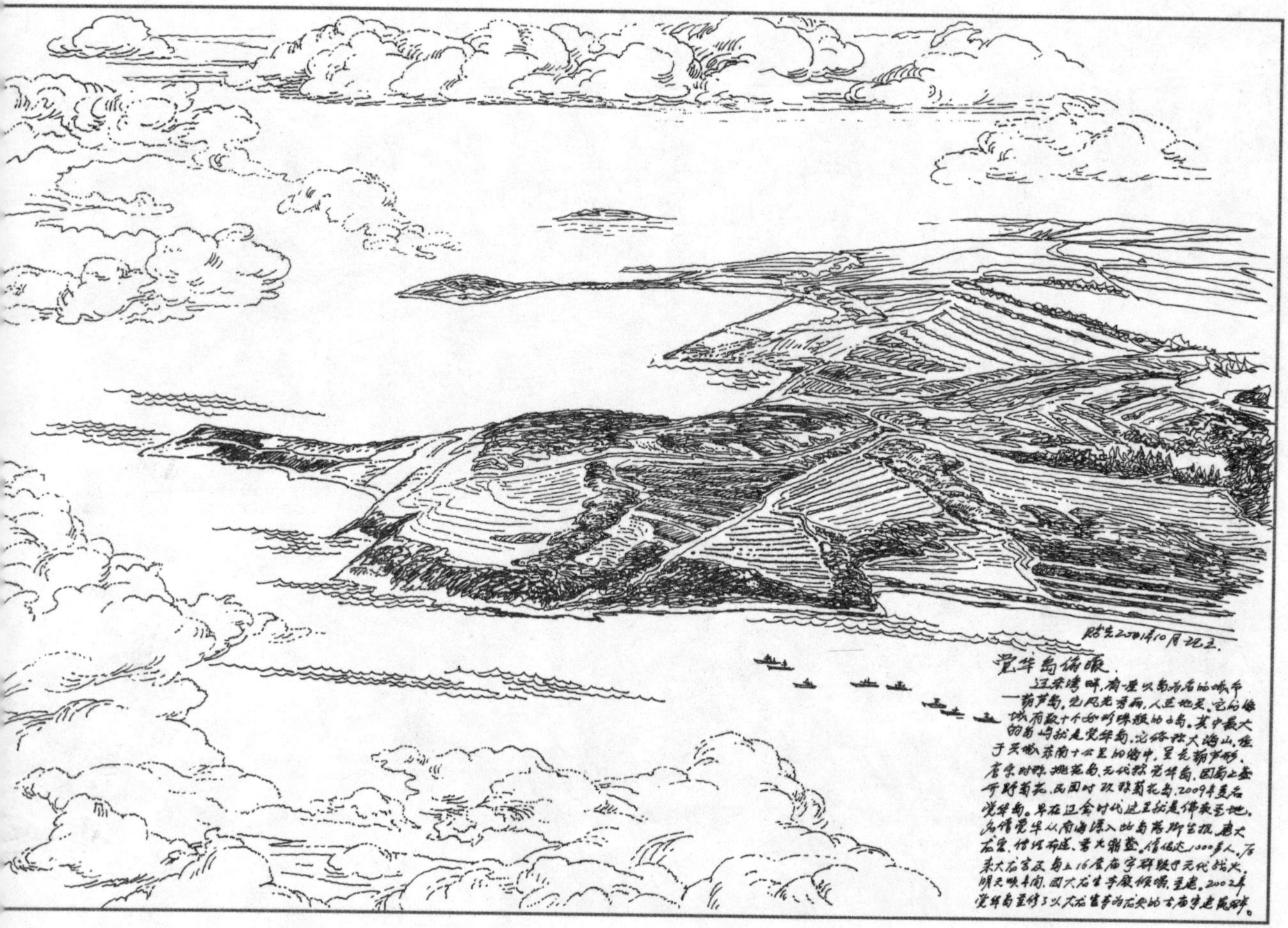

觉华岛的海岸

据地质学家考察认定，觉华岛原与大陆相连，史前时期一次大地震造成大陆架坍塌断裂，遂与大陆分离，形成岛屿。岸边多为嶙峋的礁石。

Coast of Juehua Island

According to geologists, the island was originally connected with the mainland. It separated from the mainland after a big earthquake happened in prehistoric times which collapsed a piece of continental shelf and hence the island was formed. The seashore is full of rugged rocks.

山石嶙峋，波浪轻轻，一个坦荡伟岸，一个广阔柔情。多少人喜欢这样的海境——感慨大自然造化的神奇，欣赏佳景天成的壮丽。

觉华岛海边的渔船

Fishing Boats in the Sea Off Juehua Island

海边，一个关于船的主题。一叶锚在岸边的小舟，是近焦的景物。它默无表情，回想着风采不再的历历往事。

大龙宫寺遗址

觉华岛在辽金时代曾是远近闻名的佛教圣地。辽代名僧司空大师曾居住岛上，并在岛上修建了大龙宫寺。大龙宫寺建成后成为辽代的佛教中心；大龙宫寺的住持当时被奉为国师。在佛教界，此岛有“南有普陀山，北有觉华岛”之誉。大龙宫寺于 2002 年重修，由大雄宝殿、天王殿、钟楼、鼓楼等建筑组成。

面对遗址，想象着北方佛岛昔日的辉煌。僧侣三千，菩提成荫，香烟缥缈着多少故事。

The Dalonggong Temple

Juehua Island was once a well-known holy island of Buddhism. The Dalonggong Temple on the island had became the Buddhist centre of the Liao dynasty after it was built. In the Buddhist community, this island earned a reputation in the saying "there's Mount Putuo in South China and Juehua Island in North China". Dalonggong Temple was rebuilt in 2002 and consisted of the Grand (Mahavira) Hall, the Hall of Heavenly Kings, the Bell Tower and Drum Tower.

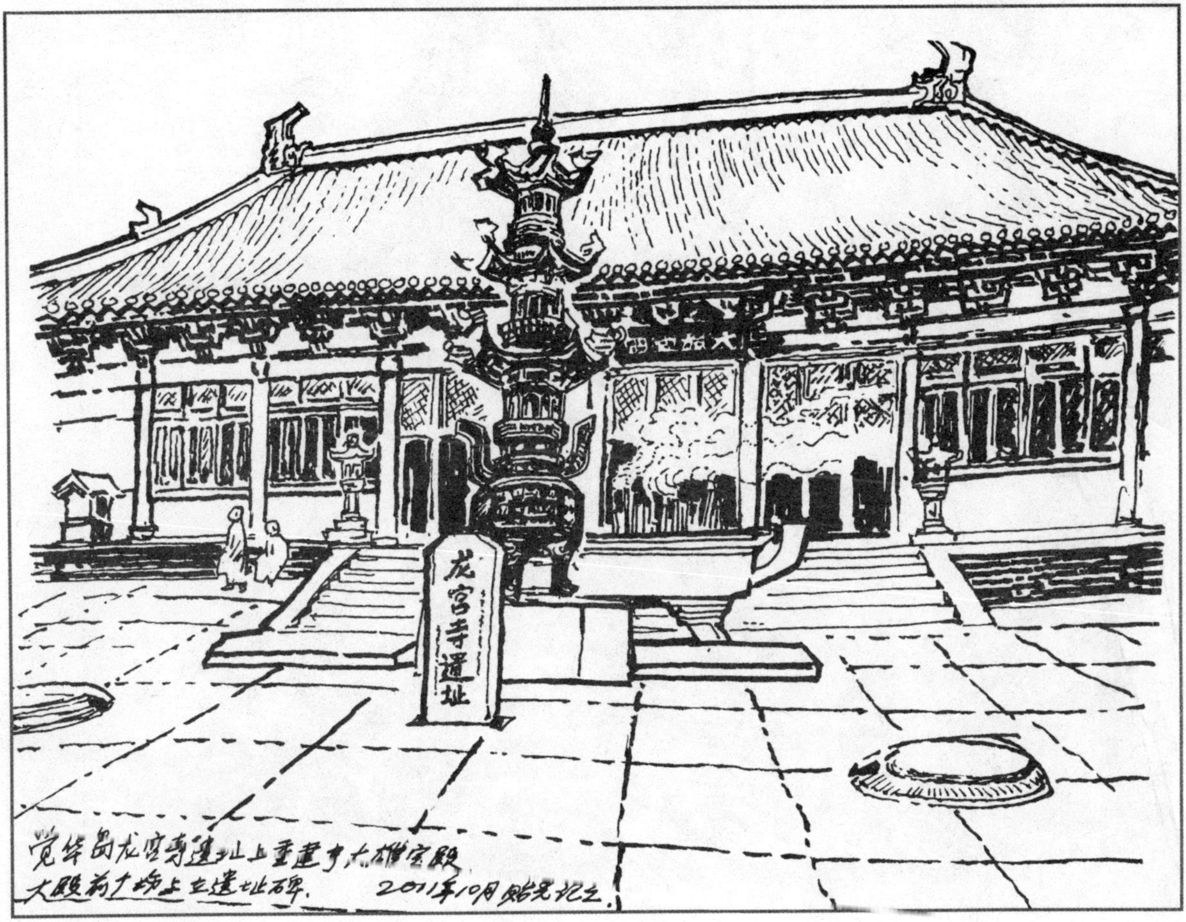

觉华岛的菩提树

菩提树，因当年释迦牟尼修行于荜拔罗树下证得菩提而被佛教徒尊为圣树。原产于印度，公元 502 年传入广州，北方很少种植，而觉华岛现有菩提树 40 余株，且树叶茂盛，能开花结果，是岛上一大奇观。

The Bodhi Trees of Juehua Island

The Bodhi Tree is regarded as the Holy Tree of Buddhism since Sakyamuni studied, meditated and was enlightened under such a tree. The Bodhi tree was originally from India and one was planted in Guangzhou in 502 A.D. They are rarely planted in North China. More than 40 Bodhi trees with flourishing leaves standing on Juehua Island has made a wonderful spectacle on the island.

你这南国的纤美，伴着晨钟暮鼓，看僧侣虔诚、香客依依；听梆磬声声、云涛拍岸，在香烟雾霭中茂盛成一片标志性的风景。

唐王洞

觉华岛上有一个深100多米的山洞，盛传燕太子丹曾在此洞避难，故称之为“藏王洞”。也称“唐王洞”，因传唐太宗李世民巡游辽东时曾在此避雨。据考证，此洞为辽代人砌造的地下通道，由巨型石板和石块砌成，口径平均1米左右，长100多米，由山顶渐低伸入大海，洞内清凉幽静。

传说往往和神话相连；名胜往往和名人相关。山洞因传说而美丽，山洞也因名人而神奇。

Tangwang Cave

There's a cave more than 100 meters deep on the island and it was an underground passageway built by ancient people with huge slates and stones. It averages 1 metre or so in diameter and is more than 100 metres in length. It gradually stretches into the sea from the top of the mountain so it's cool and secluded in the cave.

遥望觉华岛唐王洞

View of Tangwang Cave, Juehua Island from Afar

海天一色，楼枕潮汐。这是自然造化，人文神工。和谐成一幅山水画——人在画中，意在画外。

莲花山圣水寺

莲花山圣水寺始建于清康熙五十九年（1720年）。寺庙南北长104米，东西宽96米，面积约1万平方米。全寺由主院和东西跨院组成，是释、道、儒三教合一的寺庙。正门外立铁狮一对，进门是天元宫，后面是碧云宫，左右有钟鼓二楼对峙。

岩石开成莲花，小山因此得名。圣水寺，几百年，就绽放在莲花山下。

The Shengshui Temple on Lianhua Mountain

This temple was founded in 1720. It is 104 metres in length from south to north and 96 metres in width from east to west. It covers an area of about 10,000 square metres and consists of the main courtyard and east and west side courtyards. It is a temple that combines Buddhism, Taoism and Confucianism.

圣水寺天元宫

天元宫是圣水寺的大型山门楼，方座圆顶三层建筑，是遵循道教“天圆地方”之说而建。一、二层为方形，三层呈八角形，尖顶。

这里是肃穆的圣殿，当晨钟暮鼓敲醒迷惘，向往天国该是升华的崇拜。

Tianyuan Hall of the Shengshui Temple

Tianyuan Hall, a 3 storey square building with round top, is the grand entrance of Shengshui Temple. It was built following with the Taoist notion that "Heaven is round and Earth is square". The first two storeys are in square shape while the third storey is in octagonal shape. The building is crowned with a spire.

圣水寺后山坡的一座院落

正面大雄宝殿供奉佛祖释迦牟尼，东殿药师、西殿阿弥陀佛，诸多佛像都显出庄严肃穆。铁鼎香烟缭绕，钟磬叮当作响，好像到了极乐世界。西院正殿有十一面千手千眼观世音铜铸大佛，高 3.47 米，重 1.5 吨，堪称镇庙之宝。

A Courtyard on the Hillside Behind the Shengshui Temple

The main, Grand Hall enshrines Buddha Sakyamuni, while the East Hall enshrines Bhaisajyaguru Buddha and the West Hall enshrines Amitabha Buddha. Many statues of Buddha looked solemn and awe-inspiring. With incense smoke curling over the iron urn and bells clanking, visitors feel as if in paradise here. The main hall in the west courtyard enshrines a bronze statue of Avalokitesvara Bodhisattva with a thousand eyes in a thousand hands and 11 faces. The statue is 3.47 metres tall and weighs about 1.5 tons. It is regarded as the treasure of the temple.

虔诚的信徒，总想在这里寻解生活的麻团，摆脱痛苦的纠缠，祈求人生的幸福。三尺头上的神明，也总是公平地对待那些有情有意的香客，为之普降福祉。

圣水寺碧云宫

碧云宫是圣水寺的主体建筑，集城座、塔身、阁楼为一体，四层，方座大木架式建筑。古建筑专家称之为“东北古建筑什锦小品”，艺术价值很高。宫内塑有玉皇大帝、三皇五帝，四个角楼有四大天王。

在天圆地方的时空间明心见性，于是就有了这青砖高楼、红墙碧瓦、圣水悠悠、不染凡尘——北方寺院的经典。

Biyun Hall of the Shengshui Temple

The grand building is the main building of the Shengshui Temple. It is a large, 4-storey wood-framed building with square base.

【灵山寺】

灵山寺建于清乾隆三年（1738 年），于嘉庆十一年（1806 年）重修。该寺分为上下两院。共建有八角亭、慈航楼、玉皇殿、重楼、无底洞、都天殿等楼亭殿阁 29 座，是一处规模宏大的道、佛两教的古建筑群。寺院周围山岩奇异，怪石嶙峋，自然景观与人文景观交相辉映。

The Lingshan Temple

The Lingshan Temple was built in 1738. It's divided into upper and lower compounds. It consists of 29 buildings including Octagonal Pavilion, Cihang Building, Jade Emperor Hall, Chong Building, Bottomless Pit, Dutian Hall, etc. It's a large scale ancient building complex which combines Taoism and Buddhism.

林深藏古寺，宁静又致远。道教与佛教，和谐共处之。

天然寺

位于大虹螺山的西南面。最引人注目的是天然寺门外傲然屹立的两棵高大的古松。

The Tianran Temple

This temple is located in the Southwest of Mount Dahongluo. The greatest attraction lies in the two big old pine trees standing proudly outside the gate of the Temple.

天然藏古寺，钟声响青云。松涛阵阵，香烟袅袅。这里是人间清幽的一隅，这里是心灵默契的境地。